KISS

(KEEP IT SO SIMPLE)

FINANCES

FRED GREEN

To order additional copies of this book, contact:
Xlibris
1-888-795-4274
www.Xlibris.com
Orders@Xlibris.com
729507

Contents

Dedication

I dedicate this book to my father who was at least 30 years ahead of his time and taught me I could accomplish anything I set my mind to. Thanks Dad you are the Best of the Best.

Introduction

I wrote this book so that everyone who reads and works with its guide lines is truly Blessed by The Good Lord with a HAPPIER, HEALTHER & YES MORE PROSPEROUS LIFE. The book is to help you NOT MAKE THE SAME MISTAKES I HAVE. I bought my first business with $20,000.00 some 40 years ago and while there are always some bumps in the road everything just kept getting better and better till the 2008 – 2010 crash. I did all the things to save my companies, then 3, that I had always done, including reinvesting about 2 million dollars. The problem with this crash was it was really a crash and there was no recovery for almost a year and then it was very little. I ended up losing my 3 businesses, my last commercial building, 2 homes and about 10 million dollars. May the Good Lord bless everyone using this book so that what happened to me will never happen to them.

Chapter 1

I Want to Get Out of Debt

Banks and companies have told us for years that we need their credit cards. To get us interested in using these cards, they offer all kinds of incentives. Have you ever stopped and asked yourself why they are doing this? It is really quite simple: it's a huge business, and they are making lots and lots of money by getting you to use their credit cards.

Once you have the card and are using it, they tell you that you only have to pay a small amount of the total amount you owe. Are they doing that because they are your friend? Not a chance. From what I have seen on current statements, they are making 20 percent interest on the unpaid balance.

Stop for one moment and think: do you make 20 percent interest on anything you do? In most cases, I am sure the answer is no way. According to Yahoo Answers and Fox Business Take Your Pick, the average American has two to ten credit cards and owes between $1,000 and

$8,000 on them. If you're making minimum payments on your card, your monthly payment is almost all interest.

I have made every mistake, and I will tell you about each one. I cannot believe you like being controlled, and I'll bet you would like to do something about it. I have tried to make this book very, very simple to follow. Everything I pass on in *KISS Finances*, I have personally lived through.

I lost three businesses, two homes, my last commercial building, and about $10 million in the 2008–2010 crash. The federal government supported the banks, bailing them out with your taxpayer dollars. Those banks turned around and did everything in their power, which is great, to collect on loans of any kind. Let's stop and think for a moment: your tax dollars saved the banks, and now the banks are foreclosing on all kinds of properties and suing to collect on loans at a record rate. Most of the money I owed was for my business, which employed a lot of good people and built things to help the world grow.

I have two always-dos and two never-dos for you. Here's the first set: *Always* have a retirement fund, whether through work or something you contribute to on your own. Contribute, and always keep it up. *Never* use that fund for anything but your retirement. Don't let anyone—bank or person—con you out of your retirement fund.

One of the largest banks in the United States promised me—putting numerous pages in writing—that it would refinance my last commercial building if I gave them my $500,000 Roth IRA, which they could not touch in any way. I gave them that money based on the information we had in writing. Once they had the money, however, they immediately started foreclosure proceedings. After more than two years in court—the same courts we were taught are there to uphold the law—my $3-million building went to the bank, and the bank sold it to, I assume, friends for $1 million.

The point to remember here is that no one—not banks, not the government, no one—can touch your retirement fund for any reason. You should never use it for anything other than your retirement.

Now, here's the second set: *Always* pay off your home or primary home mortgage. *Never* borrow against it again. Laws vary from state to state, but you can always fight to keep your primary house.

To recap:

Your two *always-dos:*

- Have and contribute to a retirement fund.
- Pay off your primary home mortgage as quickly as you can.

Your two *never-dos:*

- Never use your retirement fund for anything but retirement.
- Never borrow against your primary house again after it is paid off.

Chapter 2

Do a Monthly Budget

Your first question about a monthly budget might be how to get started. Fortunately, budgeting is a lot easier than you might think. The worksheet and guide at the end of this chapter, which includes many of the items everyone pays monthly, will get you started.

I highly recommend that you set aside an emergency fund of at least $3,000 and preferably $5,000. By looking at your monthly budget, you can determine how quickly you can create this emergency fund. Do it as quickly as possible. Once you have those emergency dollars, put them in a separate account and do not touch them except for a true emergency. An example of a true emergency would be when the hot-water heater breaks, and you do not have the money to replace it. The money to replace the hot-water heater comes out of your emergency fund. You must replace the money as soon as you can so it's there for the next emergency. Emergencies generally arrive when we least expect them, so keep this fund up to date.

To create a budget, make a list of every penny you spend a month. Three good tools for this are your checkbook register, bank statements, and credit card statements for the last three months. Use the worksheet provided, and fill in every item you can. Now review every item that is still open. You will find a number of lines to add anything not listed. The first time you do this, you may miss some things, but it gets easier and easier each month.

Add up everything you have listed for the month and subtract that amount from your total monthly income. You now know if you are spending more than you are making, about the same as you are making, or less than you are making.

I recommend that everyone carry a piece of paper and a pen to keep track of what each person in the family spends each day, using cash, credit, or debit. This will help you improve your budget, and all family members will have a real understanding of what they are spending every month and what they are spending it on. Some may be surprised by that information.

There are a number of things I recommend using cash for. Allowances, for example—Mom's, Dad's and the children's. For family dining and entertainment, I would take actual cash and put it in envelopes at the beginning of each month. Let's say you have budgeted $300 a month for eating out as a family. Put that amount in an envelope at the beginning of each month. Every time the family goes out to eat, take that envelope to pay the bill. Once the $300 is gone, the family no longer goes out to eat that month. Do this with everyone's allowances also. All family members can spend their allowances on anything they want, but when their allowance is gone for that month, there is no more until next month.

Your Monthly Budget Worksheet

Mortgage or rent _____

Home or tenant insurance _____

Electric_____

Gas _____

Water_____

Phone _____

Cell phone_____

Cable TV _____

Internet service _____

Food at home only _____

Eating out, family only _____

Entertainment, family only _____

Allowance: Mom _____

Allowance: Dad _____

Allowance: child _____

Allowance: child _____

Car payment #1_____

Car payment #2_____

Car insurance #1 _____

Car insurance #2 _____

Car gas #1 _____

Car gas #2 _____

Car maintenance #1 _____

Car maintenance #2 _____

Clothing, adults_____

Clothing, children _____

Real estate tax on home _____

Home equity loan_____

Monthly association fee _____

Emergency fund (until fully funded) _____

Credit card #1 _____

Credit card #2 _____

Credit card #3 _____

Credit card #4 _____

_____

_____

_____

_____

_____

_____

_____

_____

_____

_____

_____

_____

_____

_____

_____

_____

_____

_____

_____

_____

_____

_____

_____

_____

_____

Chapter 3

Pay Off Your Credit Cards

Now that you have done your monthly budget, you should know if you are spending less than you make, about what you make, or more than you make.

The first thing we are going to address in getting out of debt is credit cards. Credit card issuers have romanced us for years, assuring us that the little piece of plastic they are sending us is money. *It is not money!* It is a loan, and if it is not paid back in about twenty days, the bank is going to charge you unbelievable interest on your unpaid balance (the amount not paid back). Every statement I have seen recently from anyone issuing a credit card has interest rates of 20 percent or more. You have been romanced into paying a fortune in interest if you do not pay your credit card in full when payment is due. Even if you have good credit and have a credit card or cards at a lesser rate than 20 percent, those cards are still charging 12 percent or more, and you are still paying a fortune in interest if you do not pay your account in full when payment is due.

If you read the very fine print, you will find that if you miss any payment or payments by the due date, even by one day, you will be charged an outrageous late fee—which at one time was illegal. If you pay late a few times, every credit card I have seen recently can raise your interest rate to 30 percent or more.

Now let's look at what you have to do to pay off all your credit cards. This is not as hard as you might think. At the end of this chapter, you will find a Get Me Out of Debt Worksheet. Use this to make a list of all your credit cards. Start with the cards that have the smallest balances or any cards that has a zero balance. List every credit card you have on the worksheet so that the last card you list you owe the largest amount on.

Now comes the part you will not believe, and perhaps you will not want to do. Take all of your zero-balance credit cards and cut them up. You have now taken a giant step toward getting out of debt. Once your zero-balance credit cards are gone, you know how many credit cards you have with unpaid balances. You also know how much you are currently paying per month, the rate of interest you are paying, how much of your monthly payment is interest, and how long it will take to pay a card off at the current rate you are paying. You know all of this by reviewing your Get Me Out of Debt Worksheet.

If you are making minimum payments on any of your credit cards and continue to charge on them, your monthly payment is almost all interest. If you continue to use those credit cards, your unpaid balance is going up every month. You owe more and more every month. You need to stop using all of your credit cards at once. Cut all of them up.

Every bank I am aware of now issues debit cards. If you don't have a debit card, get one from your bank. A debit card is really the cash that is in your account. Every time you use the card, you are spending your cash. The amount you charge comes out of your bank account the second you use it, just as if you took the cash out of your pocket. You are not living on credit when you use a debit card; you are spending your own cash.

At this point, I suggest you go back and review your monthly budget. There were some items that I recommended you paid in cash, such as allowances. That way, when the cash is gone, that person must wait until the next month to get more.

Now that you have stopped using your credit cards and cut them up, let's go back to the Get Me Out of Debt Worksheet and see how quickly we can pay off the cards with an outstanding balance. The reason for listing your credit cards with the smallest balance due first is because those will be the easiest to pay off. You want to take every dollar you can and use it to pay off the first credit card on your list. Keep doing this every month until the first credit card listed is totally paid off. It's okay to celebrate paying off your first credit card. Now you're going to pay off the second credit card on your list. Take the amount you were paying on your first credit card and add it to the amount you are paying on your second credit card. Pay those two amounts together every month until the second card is paid off. Keep following this procedure with every credit card you have a balance on until they are all paid in full.

If you have credit cards with large unpaid balances, I suggest you apply for a new credit card offering 0 percent interest for anywhere from twelve to eighteen months. I would do this immediately with any large unpaid-balance credit cards you have. Do this one card at a time, this time starting with the card that has the *largest* unpaid balance If you are accepted for a 0 percent credit card, transfer the total amount on your highest-balance credit card to the 0 percent credit card. Once the amount is transferred and you receive your new card, you must remember to cut it up so you are not tempted to use it.

Take the total amount you owe on your new 0 percent credit card and divide the amount you owe by the number of months you get 0 percent interest for. For example, a balance of $3,500 divided by fifteen months would equal $234 a month, rounded up to the nearest whole dollar. If you pay that amount every month for fifteen months, the 0 percent interest credit card will be paid off or paid in full, and you will have paid no interest at all on those funds. It doesn't get any better than that.

I have two examples of 0 percent credit cards currently being offered. Please be aware that any of these offers may change at any time. Chase bank is offering the Chase Slate Credit Card with fifteen months of 0 percent interest, no balance transfer fee (which some cards have), and no annual fee. Bank of America has the Bank Americard credit card with eighteen months of 0 percent interest and no annual fee. Confirm what the offer is when applying for a credit card.

Remember to cut up any new credit card you receive. If it is a 0 percent credit card, it is still a credit card, and they are just romancing you with the 0 percent term so you will use their credit card. When the 0 percent term is over, you are right back to paying 12 to 20 percent or more on all unpaid balances. Cut the credit card up when you get it.

If you are a homeowner, I have one last option for you: a home equity loan. If you can get 0 percent interest credit cards, *do not consider this option.* If you have no other way to pay off your large unpaid-balance high-interest credit cards, however, you may want to consider it. Add up all the unpaid balances on high-interest credit cards from your Get Me Out of Debt Worksheet, and take out a loan for that amount. Remember, you are only doing this to pay off your credit cards and nothing else.

Most home equity loans are for $50,000 to $100,000 or more. Do not borrow any more than you need to pay off your credit cards. Interest on a home equity loan is called *simple interest,* and it is calculated the same way as for unpaid balances on credit cards. Let's look at an example so you can see how simple interest works.

Let's say you take a $10,000 home equity loan to pay off credit cards at a 6 percent interest rate. The interest calculation on that loan would look like this:

$$\frac{\$10,000 \times .06}{360} = \$1.67 \text{ per day interest}$$

The calculation is the dollar amount of the outstanding balance times the interest rate being charged divided by the calendar days in a year. I do not know why, but banks use 360 days for this calculation. Home equity loans are billed and paid on an average every thirty days, just like credit cards. This means that at the end of thirty days, you would owe $10,050.10. When you receive your first home equity loan statement, take the total amount you were paying on all the credit cards you paid off with the loan, add to that amount if you can, and make your first loan payment.

Say you paid off seven credit cards and were paying $100 a month on each card, so you are going to pay a minimum of $700 a month or more on your first home equity loan payment. You will continue to pay this amount every month until the loan is paid in full. With the home equity loan, you will pay $50.10 in interest. If you were instead paying 20 percent interest on those credit cards, you would have paid the following:

$$\frac{\$10,000 \times .20}{360} = \$5.56 \text{ per day interest}$$

or $166.80 over thirty days. You just saved $116.70 by switching to a home equity loan.

A home equity loan is not as good as a 0 percent interest credit card, with which you would save *all* the $166.80. The interest-free credit card should be your first choice for paying off your credit cards. Please also remember that you must follow all the guidelines laid out in this chapter to be successful in paying off all of your credit cards.

If you do use a home equity loan to pay off your credit cards, make sure to close the loan account when the credit cards are paid in full. The bank or lender will do everything it can to get you to leave the account open. Don't go along with that. Close the account and destroy the checks that came with it as soon as the cards are paid in full. That way, you will not be tempted to use the account. Do this for the same reason you cut up all your credit cards.

Get Me Out of Debt Worksheet

Item	Amount Due	Monthly Payment	Interest Rate	Interest Per Payment	Will Be Paid Off

Chapter 4

Pay Off Your Car Loans

For most people, the second largest investment they make, after their home, is an automobile. America is in love with the automobile. Because of this simple fact, manufacturers have romanced us into believing that the car we drive is really a status symbol. If you are driving a Ferrari or a Bentley, maybe so. But the truth is that whether you pay $5,000 or $100,000 for your car, it still only gets you from one point to another, and it gets you there at anything from fifty miles per gallon to five miles per gallon. Usually the more expensive the car, the worse the mileage is.

If you are in the market for a car—especially a new car—dealers will tell you they are not making any money on the car at the price they are selling it to you for. That statement is totally false. Take a look at the beautiful building and facility you are in. Dealers are making a ton of money, and so is the manufacturer. If you have any kind of credit problem, you are going to pay a whole bunch of money in interest to buy a car new and even more for used.

Even with bad credit, you will get a loan, but at very high interest. If you do not make your payments, they will come and repossess your car. With poor credit, you are going to pay up to $200 a month in interest and probably not less than $100 a month on any car loan. Car loans have jumped to six years and even seven years. This is only being done to manipulate you into buying a car for a lower monthly payment.

It is estimated that the average car payment is now $447 a month. Let's think about this and do some calculations. At $100 a month, the interest payment is $7,200 for six years and $8,400 for seven years. This is just the *interest* you are paying, if you have poor credit. Your total payment, if at the average of $447 per month, would be $32,184 for six years and $37,548 for seven years.

If you have a great credit rating, you are probably still going to pay $25 to $50 a month in interest, depending on your loan amount. That is $1,800 to $3,600 in interest on a six-year loan. Before you sign on the dotted line, ask how much of your monthly payment is interest.

Let's say you have made all of your payments on time, and your loan is now paid in full. If you bought a new car, it is now six or seven years old. The mileage on the car can vary from very low to very high. The car you now own has lost 50 to 70 percent of its value. Value depends on the condition of the car and how many miles it has been driven. If the car was in an accident, that will lower the value even more. If you purchased a used car, it only gets worse.

Now let's stop for a minute and think about what kind of investment this was. If you are being honest with yourself, this was not a very good investment, and it certainly was not a good deal.

The following is an actual case history. An American-made economy car was purchased, not that many years ago, for $20,918 cash. The person who purchased the car passed about six months after the purchase. The car now had to be sold. It was virtually a brand-new car. It had less than 3,000 miles. It had never been in an accident and was garage-kept. A number of dealers were consulted, and the best price offered to purchase this six-month-old car was $10,000. The car had lost $10,918 in value in only six months.

Stop and think about this for a minute. If you are able to buy a car and pay for it, you will be saving whatever your monthly payment would have been. Using the current average monthly payment of $447 per month, that comes out to $5,364 a year. If you drove the car you bought for two years and saved the payments, you would have $10,728 to buy another car along with your trade-in. Each time you do this, it becomes easier and easier to buy a newer and/or more expensive model, if that is what you want. In the meantime, you do not have a car payment, so you are saving money—or you can apply those funds to things that need to be paid off.

At this point, if you have one or more car loans, go to the Get Me Out of Debt Worksheet at the end of Chapter

3 and list your car loan or loans. After you pay off your credit cards, take all of that money you are use to paying every month and apply it to your car loan or loans. To my knowledge, there are no auto loans out there today that have any prepayment penalties of any kind. This means that all the additional money you pay on a car loan goes directly to reducing the amount you owe on the car.

Chapter 5

Mortgages

If a bank failed during the 2008–2010 crash—and there were a great many that did—the federal government bailed it out with your tax dollars. However, if you cannot pay your mortgage, no one will come to your rescue. Banks are foreclosing and taking homes away from people at a record rate—up 81 percent in 2008. There were also record foreclosures of 2.8 million homes in 2009. As of May 19, 2011, more than 4 million people had lost their homes to foreclosure.

[*Please note:* All dollar amounts and percentages have been rounded to the nearest dollar and percent.]

Mortgage Terms

We were all romanced into believing that a thirty-year mortgage was a wonderful thing and the way to go, because the monthly payments were less. What we were not told was that out of all the payments made on a thirty-year mortgage, for the first ten years only about 32 percent of those payments actually reduce the principle balance (the amount one actually owes). The remaining 68 percent or so is interest paid to the bank or lender.

Let's look at the difference between a thirty-year mortgage and a twenty-year mortgage. If you take out a $165,000 mortgage for thirty years at an interest rate of 4.5 percent, your monthly payment would be $836. At the end of ten years, you would have reduced your principle balance—the amount you actually owe—by $32,849, leaving you a balance due of $132,149. Meanwhile, you would have already paid interest of $67,471. Please note that you have paid more than twice as much interest as principle in the first ten years of your thirty-year mortgage.

Mortgage interest is specifically designed to make banks and lenders huge amounts of money in the early years of a mortgage, as clearly shown by the example above. Please remember, you have put your house up as security to get the mortgage. If you get to a point where you cannot pay your mortgage and cannot work out a compromise with the bank, you have already given it permission to take your house. The lender can foreclose, have you vacated from the house, and sell your home to satisfy the mortgage loan.

With a twenty-year mortgage, the monthly payment is a little higher than for the thirty-year mortgage, but the savings are fantastic. The monthly payment would be $1,044. After five years—not ten years—45 percent of your payments, or $28,546, will have gone to reduce your principle, leaving you a balance of $136,454. Interest paid would be about 55 percent of your payments, or $34,987.

At the end of the next five years, your payments would have reduced the principle balance by an additional $35,732, leaving you with a balance of $100,732. The interest you paid during this second five-year period would be $26,900.

At this point, we have looked at where you would be at the end of ten years on a thirty-year mortgage and where you would be at the end of the first and second five-year periods on a twenty-year mortgage. Now we will compare the first ten years of a thirty-year mortgage to the first ten years of a twenty-year mortgage. With a thirty-year mortgage, your principle balance is $132,198. At the end of ten years on your twenty-year mortgage, your principle balance is $100,732. You owe $31,466 less on the twenty-year mortgage. You are way ahead at this point.

Let's look at the interest paid. At the end of ten years on a thirty-year mortgage, you would have paid $67,471 in interest. At the end of ten years on a twenty-year mortgage, you would have paid $61,887 in interest. Not a big savings on interest, but you are still ahead by $6,484. Please note that this confirms the earlier statement that banks and lenders make huge sums of money on interest collected in the early years of any mortgage.

Moving on to the next five years of both mortgages. On a thirty-year mortgage, you would reduce your principle balance by an additional $22,850. You now owe $109,340, and you would have paid an additional $27,302 in interest.

As you can see, your interest payment is still higher than the amount going to reduce your principle balance.

At the end of the next five years of payments on a twenty-year mortgage, you would have reduced your principle balance by $44,740 in additional payments. You now owe $55,982. You would have paid an additional $17,902 in interest. As you can see, your principle reduction was about 71 percent of your payments, more than double the amount you paid in interest.

Stop and look at what has transpired in this five-year period, and you will start to see the huge advantage of shorter-term mortgages. At the end of fifteen years on a thirty-year mortgage, you have a principle balance of $109,340. In the first fifteen years of your thirty-year mortgage, you have paid $94,772 in interest. At this point it is very easy to see that you have only reduced your principle balance by $55,714, and you have paid $94,772 in interest. What this tells you is that about 63 percent of your payments for fifteen years went to interest while only about 37 percent went toward the amount you actually owe.

At the end of fifteen years on a twenty-year mortgage, you have a principle balance of $55,982. In the first fifteen years of your twenty-year mortgage, you have paid $78,890 in interest. At the end of fifteen years, you are ahead by $53,348 in principle reduction with a twenty-year mortgage. You have paid $15,882 less in interest with a twenty-year mortgage. This once again confirms that large amounts of interest are collected in the early years of a mortgage. But you are a total of $69,230 ahead with a twenty-year mortgage.

Moving on to the next five years of both mortgages. At the end of the next five years of payments on a thirty-year mortgage, you would have reduced your principle balance by $32,938 in additional payments. You now owe $76,348. You would have paid an additional $23,908 in interest. As you can see, your interest payment is finally lower than your principle payment after twenty years of payments.

At the end of the next five years of payments on a twenty-year mortgage, you would have reduced your principle payment by $55,982. You now owe nothing; your mortgage is paid in full. You wound up paying $6,640 in interest. It is very important that you now understand that with a twenty-year mortgage, your mortgage is paid in full. You have no more mortgage payments to make, which also means you will not be paying any more interest. Please note how low your interest was in the last five years.

At the end of twenty years, you are ahead by $76,348 in principle reduction with a twenty-year mortgage. You have paid $33,150 less in interest with the twenty-year mortgage. In the last five years of your twenty-year mortgage, you are $109,498 ahead of what you would be paying with a thirty-year mortgage, and your loan is paid in full.

If you had a thirty-year mortgage, you would still have ten more years to go. You'd still owe $76,348 on your original mortgage of $165,000. Please remember, the principle balance is what you actually owe on your home. You will be paying interest on that amount for ten more years. You will pay $41,960 in interest over those ten years. Your total payments over the next ten years will be $118,308.

With a twenty-year mortgage, not only will your house be paid in full at the end of twenty years, but you will save $50,441 in interest payments. With a fifteen-year mortgage, the outlook is even better. Once again, your monthly payment is higher because of the shorter term of the mortgage. On a fifteen-year mortgage, the payment would be $1,262. We are going to look at this mortgage in three five-year segments.

At the end of the first five years of payments on a fifteen-year mortgage, you would reduce your principle balance by $43,207. You would now owe $121,793. You would have paid $32,527 in interest. Stop for a moment and take a good look at those numbers. Your principle reduction is already $10,680 greater than the amount of interest you paid.

At the end of the next five years of payments on a fifteen-year mortgage, you would have reduced your principle balance by another $54,087. You now owe $67,706. You have paid $21,648 in interest. Your principle reduction in this five-year period is 69 percent of your payment. Only 31 percent is interest.

At the end of the next five years payments on a fifteen-year mortgage, you would have reduced your principle balance by $67,706, and your house would be paid in full. You now owe nothing, and you have paid $8,029 in interest. At this point, I hope it is very clear that the shorter the mortgage term, the more you are saving in interest, and the quicker you are taking ownership of your house.

With a fifteen-year mortgage, you save $23,326 in interest over a twenty-year mortgage, and a whopping $73,768.00 over a thirty-year mortgage. Stop being romanced into a thirty-year mortgage. Wait to buy a home until you can do a twenty-year mortgage or less.

In the past, inflation was driving home prices higher and higher. Many people sold their homes and moved to bigger, more expensive ones every ten years or so. They were romanced back into a thirty-year mortgage. If they were not interested in selling and moving, banks and lenders romanced them into a new thirty-year mortgage and taking cash out. Please note, both of these things were happening because of inflation. The banks and lenders were the big winners, because homeowners were taking out a new thirty-year mortgage and starting with interest payments all over again.

Banks and lenders made huge money in interest in the first ten years of these new mortgages. If they could, they would start it all over again with new thirty-year mortgage every ten years or so They even went to interest-only payments. If you did this, you were not reducing the amount you actually owed by one penny.

The 2008–2010 crash brought the price of most homes down by almost 50 percent, and in some cases even more. This plunge in home prices trapped millions of Americans who owed more than their homes were now worth. Tens of thousands lost their jobs, their businesses, and much of what they owned. Those who were lucky enough to keep their jobs faced large reductions in their income. This led to a record number of foreclosures.

If you currently own a home and have a mortgage, consider asking your bank or lender for an amortization schedule. You should be able to get this the day you request it. What this schedule will tell you is every payment you will make and how much of that payment is going to interest and how much is going to reduce principle (the actual amount you owe). If your current mortgage is more than twenty years and at an interest rate of more than 4 percent, you should ask about a loan modification. Look at doing a twenty-year mortgage or, better yet, a fifteen-year mortgage. Request amortization schedules for these or any mortgage you are considering to help you decide which is best for you. As you have seen from my examples, you are going to save a huge amount by doing a shorter mortgage.

Programs to Help

If you own a home and you are in an "underwater" mortgage or lost your job and are unemployed, there are programs to help you. *Underwater mortgage* means you now owe more for your house than it is worth because of the crash. If you have an underwater mortgage, there are programs set up to help you in every way they can. They include the following:

- *Home affordable refinance program (HARP).* If you are current on your mortgage but cannot get it refinanced because the value of your house has declined, you may be eligible to refinance through HARP. The program is designed to help you refinance into a new affordable mortgage.

- *Principle reduction alternative (PRA).* This program was designed to help homeowners whose homes are worth significantly less than they owe by encouraging the mortgage holder(s) to reduce the amount owed on the home.

- *Treasury/FHA second lien program (FHA2LP).* If you have a second mortgage and the holder of your first mortgage agrees to participate in a Federal Housing Administration (FHA) short refinance, you may qualify to have your second mortgage on the same home reduced or eliminated through FHA2LP. If the holder of your second mortgage agrees to participate, the total amount of your mortgage debt cannot exceed 115 percent of your home's current value.

If you are an unemployed homeowner, the following programs are set up to help you in every way they can:

- *Home Affordable Unemployment Program (UP).* If you are having a hard time making your mortgage payments because of unemployment, you may be eligible for this program. UP can provide a temporary reduction or even a suspension of your mortgage payments for at least twelve months while you look for a new job.

- *Emergency Homeowner Loan Program (EHLP).* As I understand it, this is available on a state-by-state basis. You will need to check with the state you live in to see if assistance is available.
- *FHA special forbearance.* If you are having a hard time paying your mortgage because of unemployment and have no other income, you may be eligible for an FHA special forbearance. FHA now requires mortgage holders to extend a forbearance period. The mortgage holder can offer a reduced or suspended mortgage payment for up to twelve months to FHA borrowers who qualify for the program.

Please note all of these programs are subject to change. If interested please confirm they are still available and what the terms are.

Short Sale, Deed in Lieu, and Redemption

We are now going to look at three options you can consider for a home or property. Please note, I am not a lawyer or a realtor. If you would like to look into any of these options, you will need to hire those professionals. I would talk to two or three in each category. Make sure to ask if they have a lot of experience in the area you are interested in, what their fees are, and how they collect those fees.

The three possibilities you will want to look into are short sale, deed in lieu, and redemption on a foreclosed home. I have personal experience with the first two, and the information I am passing on to you is based on those experiences. The information on redemption is based on research on that subject.

So what is a *short sale* and why would you do it? You would usually do a short sale because the home is now worth far less than the money owed on it. During the inflation years, you may have been romanced into refinancing and taking money out, or taking out a second mortgage, or getting a home equity loan. Now you owe far more than your home is worth. If you wish to consider a short sale, it has been my experience that once the short sale is completed, you owe $0 on that home.

I am sure that sounds wonderful. But remember, you will need a lawyer and a realtor who have a lot of experience with short sales. All of your lenders must agree to the sale. If you have two or even three loans on your home, every one of those lenders has to agree to the short sale. This can be a long and trying experience. **You are losing your home and all of your payments along with your down payment,** The realtor you choose should handle all of this.

In the past, lenders were giving sellers $3,000 for relocation. They can offer you any amount—one of mine said $20,000 on a limited-time bases. I responded at once (you must respond through your relator), and the program had ended apparently before it even began. A lender could send you a 1099 for the amount of money it is writing off. If it does, you could be liable for income tax for that amount of money. You need to work with your lawyer to see that this does not happen—or that if it does, you will not have any income tax due on that amount.

Next, let's look at *deed in lieu*. Once again, you will need a lawyer who has a lot of experience in foreclosures. What you are agreeing to when you do a deed in lieu is giving your lender the deed to your property in lieu of any further payments. You are losing your home and all the payments along with your down payment in exchange for owing nothing else on the property. Before you agree to this, your lawyer needs to make sure the lender has no further recourse on the property and that you now owe nothing—the lender cannot collect another penny from you for this property. Once again, the lender could send you a 1099 for the amount you no longer owe, and you might owe income tax on that amount. You need your lawyer to tell you if this could happen and if you will in fact owe any taxes.

For the third option, *redemption on a foreclosed home*, you will once again need a lawyer who has a lot of foreclosure experience. There is a period of time with a home that has already been sold at a foreclosure sale when you can still reclaim the house. To do this, you would need to pay the outstanding mortgage balance in full along with any and all costs of the foreclosure.

Reverse Mortgage

Depending on your age, you may be romanced into a reverse mortgage. This is *not* a mortgage in the sense that we've been discussing in this chapter. It is really just a loan to senior homeowners. One of the many qualifications is that all homeowners must be at least sixty-two. This is a loan, and you must pledge the equity of your home as collateral to get this loan. If you own your home free and clear, you are now putting it up to get this loan, and the loan will have to be paid back.

Reverse mortgages are being sold to seniors as an income stream. This is not income as you would know it. Every dollar you receive on a reverse mortgage is a loan against your home, and you are paying interest on that loan. This loan and all the accumulated interest must eventually be paid back. If you wanted to move, the loan would have to be paid back in full. Usually the loan does not have to be repaid until the last owner moves out of the house or passes away. At that time, the person who moved or the estate has about five months to repay the total amount due on the reverse mortgage.

The home can be sold to pay off the loan. If the home is sold, the person who moved or the estate gets all the funds that are not needed to pay off the reverse mortgage. If the last person living in the home has passed away, his or her estate has to sell the home to pay off the reverse mortgage. If the home sells for less than the amount due on the loan, the estate is not liable for any amount due after the sale is complete.

There are many requirements for a reverse mortgage. The FHA requires that all the homeowners be at least sixty-two years old. They have to own the home with no loans against it, or if there are any loans against the home, they must be covered and paid off by the reverse mortgage. If there is still a mortgage on the home, it too must be covered and paid off by the reverse mortgage.

Let's look at an example of what this means. You have a loan of $25,000 and you still have a mortgage with a balance due of $52,000. At this point, you still owe a total of $77,000 on your home. The current market value of your home is $295,000. You and your spouse are at least sixty-two years old, and you own the house together.

So far, so good. But you must also meet financial requirements that are set up by the Federal Department of Housing and Urban Development (HUD). Among other things, you must be able to maintain your home by paying all property charges, including real estate taxes and insurance. You must also live in the home.

If you decide to do a reverse mortgage, how much will you receive if you are accepted?

The amount of the loan (you must understand that this is a loan against your house) usually depends on four things:

1. The appraised value of your home when you apply
2. Your age
3. Current interest rates
4. Government-imposed lending limits

I would only consider a reverse mortgage if you are retired, truly need more funds to live on, and have no other choice. At this point, you must remember that a reverse mortgage is not a conventional mortgage—it is a loan on which interest is charged every month and added to the amount you owe. The interest keeps adding up until the loan is paid in full. Reasons to avoid a reverse mortgage include the following:

- Your heirs will not get the house if they can't pay off the loan.
- Fees on the loan are usually high.
- Interest rates are usually higher than for a traditional home equity loan.
- You are still responsible for all the costs of upkeep on the home.

Reverse mortgages have very few good points. If you are thinking about a reverse mortgage or have applied for one, I suggest you consult someone who is very knowledgeable about them—but not the person or the group making the loan to you. Banks and lenders make lots and lots of money on reverse mortgages. You would be wise to discuss this loan with an accountant and/or an attorney.

Banks Are Not Your Friends

Banks and lenders are not giving you a loan because they are your friends. They make money on mortgages of all kinds. At this point, you may be asking yourself if banks ever get in trouble doing mortgages. The answer to that is yes, they do.

One recent example involves Citibank, which in July of 2014 agreed to pay $7 billion to settle charges that it packaged bad mortgages during the real estate boom before the financial crisis. Under the terms of the settlement, the bank admitted to its misdeeds in great detail.

What the settlement meant to Citibank was that the bank was able to avoid civil suits by the Justice Department. This settlement was very similar to agreements with JP Morgan Chase Bank as well as other banks and lenders in this same time frame.

Citibank lost $3.8 billion in the settlement, which was essentially equal to its earnings for that quarter (ninety days). If you are feeling sorry for Citibank, it is really not necessary. The year before, Citibank made $14 billion and had $35 billion in cash on its balance sheet as of June 30.

Attorney General Eric Holder and many other financial experts have stated that the mortgage crisis was a very large contributor to the financial crisis that devastated our economy in 2008–2009. It is estimated that over a trillion dollars disappeared from our economy in this crash. Personally, I lost two homes, my last commercial building, three businesses, and about $10 million.

Let's sum up this chapter. If you are in the process of buying a home or even thinking about it, or are in the process of redoing a current mortgage, please reread this chapter and understand that it would be in your best interest for it to be fifteen years or less, and never more than twenty years.

If you currently have a mortgage, go to the Get Me Out of Debt Worksheet at the end of Chapter 3 and list your mortgage. If you have additional loans on your home, such as a home equity loan, list all of them on your worksheet as well.

Chapter 6

You Need to Give to Receive— What Goes Around Comes Around

Your first thought when you look at this chapter may be, "What does this have to do with my finances?" Well, I am here to inform you, after forty years in my own businesses, that both of these sayings have as much to do with your finances as any other chapter in this book—perhaps even more.

I think when most of us hear "You need to give to receive," we immediately think about money. There are a lot of organizations and churches that are doing many, many wonderful things all around the world, and they ask us all to donate funds to support them in their many causes. I believe everyone who has an income will find it very rewarding to contribute to charitable organizations or churches that go out of their way to help others who are less fortunate and in need of help.

You can also contribute by volunteering your time and expertise. There are numerous organizations that need volunteers on a regular basis to help people in need. The numerous food pantries all across the US that provide food to people who cannot afford to buy it themselves are always in need of volunteers. I currently volunteer one day a week at Willow Creek Church's Care Center.

Churches have many other things that they need volunteers for. Hospitals have a number of things that they do that involve volunteers, as do many local organizations that are out there helping others. Giving of yourself and your time is just as important as contributing funds to support a cause you believe in. You will find that volunteering is as rewarding and perhaps even more so than donating funds.

You can, of course, give your time and/or funds to an individual you know who is in need of help. You can also donate things you no longer wear or use. My rule of thumb for this is that if I have not worn it or used it in a year or more, it is something I should definitely think about giving away. There are a very large number of charities and stores like Goodwill that welcome your donations— and will give you a receipt for your items that you can deduct from your income tax, if you qualify. You will get paid back many times over for doing these good deeds, in ways that you might never imagine.

Now let's look at "What goes around comes around." Work on doing the following three things, and in time, you will find that they come back to you over and over again, even better than you could ever imagine. You will find that these things will lead you to a happier, healthier, more productive life:

- Always be the best at everything you do.
- Always give 110 percent to everything you do, from cleaning up the yard to the job you go to every day to earn a living.
- Stay positive while you are doing your best and giving your all.

If you try your best to do these things every day, you can expect good things to happen to you, and they will. People may not tell you, but everyone will notice your positive attitude and sincere effort, from your boss to your coworkers to your neighbors and family members.

This doesn't mean that things are never going to happen that upset you. What matters is how you deal with the situation when it comes. Let's take something as simple as getting a flat tire. You may think *I can't believe this* and then get out of the car and change it and be on your way. If you know this is something you cannot do, you can call the auto club to get someone to come change the tire. Getting mad, yelling, swearing, having a temper tantrum, and kicking the flat all accomplish nothing, except probably upsetting you more. The situation here is quite simple: you have a flat tire, so change it or have it changed and be on your way.

The bigger the problem is, the more difficult it is to act rationally and keep your wits about you. I owned three businesses; two of them I had owned for many years, and they had weathered every financial storm, recovered, and in a relatively short period of time did better than they had before the storm. My newest business, which was about eight years old, had paid its dues and was well on its way to being a strong profitable company. In the 2008–2009 crash, all three businesses stopped over night. The businesses had done well over the years, and every downturn in the past, I had dealt with. I supported my companies with my own funds, and they recovered in a reasonable period of time. Because of that past experience, I supported all three of my businesses in this latest crash.

What turned out to be very, very different this time is that our entire economy collapsed. Almost all homes lost 50 percent or more of their value. Most stocks lost 50 percent or more of their value. In my area, the Western Suburbs of Chicago, commercial real estate lost 50 percent or more of its value. This was something I had never seen in all my years of business. Businesses did not recover in a reasonable period of time. It took over a year to see any recovery, and then it was minimal.

After supporting my business with over $2 million of my own funds—which meant selling everything I had that was liquid, including my ROTH IRA—I ran out of money. I ended up losing my three businesses, my last commercial building, two homes, and about $10 million. One of the things this experience has prompted me to do is write this book to help all its readers and as many people in the world as I can to avoid the mistakes I made. Please remember, "The glass is always at least half full," and things are always going to get better. I believe that if you follow the guidelines in this book, you will get to that better place in life and be happier, healthier, and yes—more prosperous.

Give of yourself and your funds to help others who are in need of help. Always give 110 percent to everything you do. By doing this, you will learn and grow faster and better that you could ever imagine. No matter what happens along the way, stay positive and dedicated to everything you are doing, and you can expect good things to come to you. These may even far exceed your expectations.

May the Good Lord Bless every person who reads and follows the guide lines of this book.

CPSIA information can be obtained
at www.ICGtesting.com
Printed in the USA
LVOW10s1750141116

512905LV00001B/229/P

9 781514 485712